SO YOU WANT TO BE A MORTGAGE BROKER

DBD665903

LEARN HOW TO...

SUCCESSFULLY ENTER THE MORTGAGE BROKERAGE BUSINESS
GET STARTED QUICKLY AND EASILY
MAKE MORE MONEY THAN YOU EVER DREAMED, WHILE WORKING FEWER HOURS

AMEEN KAMADIA

addition to your commission. What you negotiate with your boss is up to you. But if you are making the company money, they will want to keep you and should increase your compensation.

The new trend in the industry is to offer brokers 100% commission. Every company has its own guidelines, but under this plan, you keep the entire Origination Fee and any YSP. The company gets a set fee per loan and also a desk fee per month. These companies offer almost no training, so it might not be a good idea to start at one of these places, but once you get going, you might consider it. It is almost the same as opening your own company, but without the overhead.

Check the Internet job boards for any openings in your area. Websites like monster.com list hundreds of jobs available in the real estate financing industry.

Is My Job Secure?

Very secure. A job as a mortgage broker is the most secure job you can have—especially since you work on commission. If you do not produce, they do not have to pay you. You also do not eat. So it is a good idea to produce as much as you can. Your job relies entirely on your willingness to work. Your job security will always be totally in your own hands.

Mortgage companies come and go. The one you work for might fail and go out of business. It doesn't matter. There are a thousand others that will love to hire you. The key is production. If you produce loans, you will have people throwing incentives at you to get you to work for them.

You never have to worry about being laid off again. And if you set your business up the right way, you do not have to worry about the ups-and-downs of the economy. People will always have to move, buy and sell their houses. And in today's easy finance society, no one pays cash for homes anymore. So every time someone sells a house, there is need for a mortgage.

CAN I DO THIS PART-TIME?

Sure. In fact, if you already have a stable job that earns you a good income you should probably start off part-time first. See how you like the business. Once you start making enough, you can make the jump into full-time. That's how most people do it anyway. Anytime you start a new job it is a risk. And in this case, there is no stable paycheck to rely on.

So common sense dictates that you either, start part-time until you are making enough in commissions to support yourself and your family, or you have enough in the bank to support you for a few months, until you start earning.

There are many brokers who started out part-time and then graduated to full-time status. And there is not much that cannot be done at night or on the weekends. The processing will be done by the processors in your office.

One of the reasons that brokers actually go to peoples' homes to get applications signed is because they are part-time. If you are full-time, you would want the borrowers to come to your office. Psychologically, it works in your favor. But if you cannot do that, meet wherever you have to, to get the loan.

Keep in mind that borrowers will not like it if they find out that you are not full-time. Since buying a house is a big deal to most people, they would rather have an experienced professional. That's just human nature. So be sure that you do not volunteer the fact that you are part-time.

Another thing to keep in mind is, loans take a long time to close. And you do not get paid until they close. The average loan takes up to 30 days to close. Once you take the application, you still have to wait another month until you see any money. You need to have enough loans closing so that if you do not get paid for 2-3 weeks you will still be OK.

CHAPTER 5

Opening Your Own Company

Once you get a hang of the business and start producing several loans a month, you might decide to open your own company.

Borrowers like it even more when they know they are dealing with the owner of the company and not just an employee.

Starting your own company is not as hard as it sounds either. You will already know how to get loans, and you should have a good idea how to process them. Or you can hire a processor. The hardest part is finding lenders. But if you have been in the business, you will meet and get to know the lender representatives, and they will be happy to help you get approved with them once you go out on your own.

Another way to find lenders is by looking through mortgage magazines, like the ones mentioned in this book. They all have ads from lenders looking for brokers. Or you can check out the websites of the National Association of Mortgage Brokers, and your state association. They will most likely have ads of lenders, and many lenders will be members.

The overhead can be minimal. Rent and employees will be your largest expenses. You will also need to spend money for advertising, but you were probably doing that working for someone else anyway.

The biggest reward is not having to split the commission. Going from a 50% commission split to owning to keeping 100% because it's your own company is like doing twice as many loans.

How soon you can open your own company depends on your state regulations. Some states let you open right away. Others require you to work in the industry for a certain amount of time before you can open your own.

One concept that has been catching on lately is Net Branching. This is where a lender wants to open offices, but does not want to spend the money. So they let you open an office for them.

You become an employee of theirs, and manage your office. You are allowed to run it anyway you want, and your compensation is based on the net profits of the office. They let you use their corporate name and all their lenders or they can fund your loans themselves.

As net branching became popular companies started calling themselves: net branches, branch affiliates, virtual loan originators, interactive partners, partner branches, affiliate branching, and retail branch network. They all pretty much mean the same thing.

Net Branching is one step away from working for someone else and one step away from owning your own company. It's right in the middle of both.

The one downside of opening your own company is that it is hard to get approved to do FHA and VA loans. You have to go through a strict approval process with both agencies. And the requirements are strict. Many smaller mortgage brokers do not bother, and only do conventional and sub-prime loans.

But if you choose Net Branching, you can do both FHA and VA from day one if the company is already approved, and it should be.

Some other benefits of net branching include:

- The ability to close loans as a broker or a banker
- No state requirements to meet to open an office
- Fewer disclosures to give to bowers
- If you close a loan as a Banker, the borrower will never know how much you earned for the Yield Spread Premium. As a broker they will
- The company provides accounting and payroll services
- Group benefits
- Legal and compliance support
- Marketing help
- Computer and technology help

Some of the disadvantages are:

- They get a portion of the commission on each loan
- You are an employee and have to go by their guidelines—including hiring and firing personnel
- If the company fails, you have nothing
- If you choose the wrong net branch, and want to cancel the agreement, you have to start over with a new company name and expenses
- Most of the good ones, require you to have experience and production before they will work with you

CHAPTER 6

How Do I Get Started?

BASIC REQUIREMENTS

The requirements vary from state-to-state. But they are generally the same.

You must be at least 18 years old and able to enter into contracts. So you must be of sound mind. Also, if your state has licensing, you will have to be fingerprinted and your background will be checked before a license will be issued.

In some states, you will need to pass an exam before you get your license. They want to be sure you have some idea of what you are doing before you start.

In most states, you will have to take a class, which may have a test at the end, which you will be required to pass. These classes are more like driving school than the SAT, so even if you sleep through the whole thing, you probably will still pass.

WHAT DO I DO FIRST?

The first thing you do is some homework. Don't make a face, it's not hard. Get on your computer and do a search for your state's banking department.

Look for any reference to mortgage licenses. Or you can just do a search for "(your state) mortgage license" Through these searches you will find the website that will provide the most up-to-date and detailed instructions on exactly what you need to do.

As of the date this is being written, 45 states have laws requiring mortgage broker licenses. But most do not require that individuals have licenses. Only companies are required to have a license. Texas and Florida are the two largest that require everyone working in the business to have a license. More states will follow these two.

Check below for your state:

Alabama
www.bank.state.al.us

Alaska
www.dced.state.ak.us/bsc/mortgagelender.htm

Arkansas
www.accessarkansas.org

Arizona
www.azbanking.com

California
www.dre.cahwnet.gov

Colorado
www.ago.state.co.us

Connecticut
www.state.ct.us/dob/pages/1stmtg.htm

Delaware
www.state.de.us/bank/applyfor.htm
www.state.de.us/bank/mbintro.htm

District of Columbia
www.obfi.washingtondc.gov/services/mortgage_app.shtm

Florida
www.dbf.state.fl.us/licensing/MBlist.html

Georgia
www.ganet.org.dbf
www.ganet.org/cgibin/pub/ocode/ocgsearch?docname=OCode/
G/7/3/5&highlight=7-3-5

Hawaii
www.state.hi.us/dcca/
www.capitol.hawaii.gov/hrscurrent/Vol10/hrs454/HRS_454-3.htm

Idaho
www2.state.id.us/finance/dof.htm

Indiana
www.in.gov/pla/
www.inamb.com/education.asp

Illinois
www.obre.state.il.us/
www.obre.state.il.us/RESFIN/mortbank.htm

Iowa
www.idob.state.ia.us/

Kansas
www.osbckansas.org/DOCML/docmllawsandregs.html

Kentucky
www.dfi.state.ky.us/
http://162.114.4.13/KRS/288-00/CHAPTER.HTM

Louisiana
www.ofi.state.la.us/
www.ofi.state.la.us/lcclidx.htm

Maine
www.state.me.us/pfr/ccp/ccphome2.htm
http://janus.state.me.us/legis/statutes/9-A/title9-Ach00sec0.html

Maryland
www.dllr.state.md.us/license/fin_reg/mortlend/mdfinreg.html
http://mlis.state.md.us/cgi-win/web_statutes.exe

Massachusetts
www.state.ma.us/dob/

Michigan
www.cis.state.mi.us/fis/ind_srch/mortgage/mortgage_industry_
criteria.asp

Minnesota
www.commerce.state.mn.us/mainfe.htm
www.revisor.leg.state.mn.us/stats/58/

Mississippi
www.dbcf.state.ms.us/
www.dbcf.state.ms.us/slregs98sept.htm

Missouri
www.ecodev.state.mo.us/finance/
www.moga.state.mo.us/STATUTES/C367.HTM

Montana
www.commerce.state.mt.us/Bnk&Fin/index.html

Nebraska
www.ndbf.org/fin.htm
www.ndbf.org/mb-act.pdf

Nevada
www.fid.state.nv.us/
www.leg.state.nv.us/NRS/NRS-645B.html

New Hampshire

g

iv.htm
-bin/...

New Mexico

www.rld.state.nm.us/fid/index.htm

www.rld.state.nm.us/fid/laws/otherregs.htm

New York

www.banking.state.ny.us

http://assembly.state.ny.us/leg/?cl=9

North Carolina

www.banking.state.nc.us/

www.banking.state.nc.us/gs/gs53a15.htm

North Dakota

www.state.nd.us/bank/

http://ranch.state.nd.us/LR/cencode/CCT47.pdf

Ohio

www.com.state.oh.us/ODOC/dfi/

Oklahoma

www.okdocc.state.ok.us

www.okdocc.state.ok.us/introMB.htm

Oregon

www.cbs.state.or.us/external/dfcs/mortgage/mortmain.htm

Pennsylvania

www.banking.state.pa.us/

www.banking.state.pa.us/PA_Exec/Banking/resource/acts.htm

Rhode Island

www.state.ri.us/manual/data/queries/stdept_.idc?id=100

www.rilin.state.ri.us/Statutes/TITLE19/19-14-2/INDEX.HTM

South Carolina

www.state.sc.us/consumer/

South Dakota

www.state.sd.us/dcr/bank/BANK-HOM.htm

http://legis.state.sd.us/statutes/Index.cfm

ıessee
ıw.state.tn.us/financialinst/
ıww.state.tn.us/sos/rules/0180/0180.htm

Texas
www.tsld.state.tx.us/
www.tsld.state.tx.us/adoptedrulcs.htm

Utah
www.commerce.state.ut.us/re/
www.commerce.state.ut.us/re/mortgage/mortregfaq.htm

Vermont
www.bishca.state.vt.us
www.bishca.state.vt.us/BankingDiv/lenderapplic/PROCED.PDF

Virginia
www.state.va.us/scc/division/banking/index.htm

Washington
www.wa.gov/dfi/cs/mb.htm
www.wa.gov/dfi/cs/rcw19146.htm

West Virginia
www.wvdob.org/professionals/n_mortgage.htm

Wisconsin
www.wdfi.org/fi/mortbank/
www.wdfi.org/fi/mortbank/mbfaqs.htm#2

Wyoming
http://audit.state.wy.us/banking/

Another way to check is to visit **www.namb.org**. This is the website of the National Association of Mortgage Brokers. They also list the states that need licenses and each state's licensing website.

You can also visit the following site for this info: **http://www.thomas-law.com/mtgbrokers.html**

Your second step is to get your own license if you Take a class if you have to. Most real estate schools offer mortgage classes. You can also go to your local community college. They almost always offer classes in real estate.

Your state might have you take a competency test. Pass with a certain percentage and you get your license. But if you don't pass, don't worry. Study harder and try again. And keep taking the test until you do pass.

If your state has individual licenses, mortgage classes and tests can cost you about $500.

Third, get a job. In Texas, you have to find a company to sponsor you before you can take the state test. So after you pass, you would work for this company. Elsewhere you can look for a job while you are preparing for the state test, or as soon as you decide to become a mortgage broker. Getting a job and finding a company to work for has been discussed in another section.

Fourth, get an understanding of the job. Get all the forms and familiarize yourself with them. Get a copy of Residential Mortgage Loan Origination Made Easy from our website. Learn your company's policies and procedures. Take any training classes your company offers. And once you become a member of your local Association of Mortgage Brokers, you can take their training classes as well.

That's about it. The hardest part is deciding to take the plunge. Once you decide to become a mortgage broker the rest is easy.

How Long Does It Take To Start?

It depends on your state's laws. If you have to get your own license it could take up to 3 months. If not, you can be in the business in one day.

WHAT DO I HAVE TO KNOW?

Actually nothing. You will learn everything you need as you go along. If you already have knowledge of the process, it will help you shorten the learning curve. If not, resources like this book will help you become a pro in no time.

Make sure you thoroughly understand the concepts discussed in this book. Pay attention to:

- What brokers do
- How they get paid
- The loan process
- The requirements to become a broker

After you decide that you want to become a broker, follow the steps outlined in this chapter. Then, after you become a broker, that's when the fun starts.

Marketing and loan origination are the two things you will be focused on. Getting people to come to you, trust you, and let you do their loan is what this business is all about.

CHAPTER 7

Would You Make a Good Broker?

• TAKE THIS TEST TO SEE

The following test is designed to get you to think about your likes and dislikes, to see if you are a good candidate to be a mortgage broker.

1. Do you want to be your own boss?
2. Would you rather skip the morning rush hour commute to a job every morning?
3. Are you willing to work on weekends?
4. Do you like working with people?
5. Can you use a calculator and basic software programs?
6. Will you be OK mentally with not earning a steady paycheck?
7. Can you discipline yourself to work a set schedule, even though no one is watching?
8. Can you budget your income?
9. Can you work nights in the beginning?
10. Can you handle rejection?
11. Are you willing to constantly keep learning?
12. Are you willing to spend money on your education?
13. Will you be comfortable asking people you know for business?

14. Can you stay focused and determined so you can withstand the ups–and-downs of the business?

15. Will you stick with it, even when the going gets a little rough?

16. Do you want to be a white-collar worker?

17. Are you an ethical person?

18. Can you be trusted with peoples' confidential and private information?

19. Do you work well with others?

20. When given responsibility, do you give it 100% effort?

21. Do you know a large number of people you can approach for business?

22. Have you ever studied marketing?

23. Are you willing to learn how to do marketing?

24. Are you willing to learn how to be a great salesperson?

25. Does the thought of earning what you are worth excite you?

These are the qualities you need to be a good mortgage broker. The more "Yes" answers you gave the better.

Being a mortgage broker brings a lot of responsibility. Your actions can cause a lot of good or a lot of harm to your clients. Before you enter this business, make sure this is what you really want to do. Just like any other job, you will have to work hard to earn a living, but the rewards are great.

CHAPTER 8

The Loan Process

The loan process becomes child's play after you go through it a few times. But for the borrowers, it can be a daunting challenge.

It all starts with a rate quote. Generally, a potential borrower will tell you he is looking for a loan and ask what your rates are. A more sophisticated borrower will ask you for a Good Faith Estimate of your rate and all your fees.

In order to provide this information, you will have to know what type of loan he wants and what his credit looks like. Only then can you start quoting rates.

But let's say the guy likes whatever you told him and wants to move forward. The next step is to fill-out the loan application, also known as the 1003. You will also gather any needed information to help him qualify. (Our company also requires a check for the appraisal and credit report at this time.)

Once you have all this, you turn it over to the processor who starts working her magic. She puts the loan package together. She orders the appraisal and credit reports. She locks the loan in case you didn't already. She makes all the necessary copies and forwards them to the lender.

At the lender's, it takes the file a few days to get through underwriting. Once it does, the underwriter faxes a conditions sheet back to the processor. Most items will be OK, but there are a couple documents still needed. So the processor calls the borrower to obtain these extra documents. She then forwards them to the underwriter, who then agrees to fund the loan.

The processor then calls the title company to open title and arrange for closing. Once the money is wired from the lender to the title company, closing can take place. In the meantime, the borrower has to show proof that he obtained homeowner's insurance on the house.

If everything is OK and the title is clear, the closing can take place, usually at the title company's office. All the documents are signed by the borrower and the loan is closed.

The title company will mail or courier your fees to your office and your office will write your check for your commission.

WHAT EXACTLY DOES THE PROCESSOR DO?

Most mortgage companies have processors. These people do the paperwork on the loan. The mortgage broker's main role is the get the loan and get the borrowers to agree to it. The processor then takes over and processes all the information, making it presentable to the lender.

The processor enters the 1003 and disclosures into the computer. She locks the loan; orders the appraisal and credit report; gathers all verifications; asks for any other needed info from the borrowers; satisfies any conditions of the lender; orders title and survey; and then arranges the closing.

But if you're smart, you won't just turn the file over to the processor and disappear. If the processor needs info from the borrowers, either she can get it or you can. It is better if you do it. They know you and trust you. In their minds, it will appear that you are involved in all aspects of their loan, and that is exactly how we want it to seem. Whatever the processor needs, get it for her right away. Take an active interest in your loans. It's surprising, but many brokers lose interest after they turn the file over to processing. They only help out when the loan is in trouble. (It wouldn't be in trouble, if they'd stayed involved!) You worked so hard to get the loan, don't let anyone else drop the ball on your commission.

What Does An Underwriter Do?

The underwriter works for the lender. Once the paperwork is processed and the file is sent to the lender, the underwriter takes over and makes sure all the information is there so she can approve the loan. If something is missing or she needs more verifications, she will make those conditions of the loan. Until you supply her with the needed info, the loan will not be approved.

Some brokers see the underwriter as the enemy. Sometimes you will too. But underwriters are people just like you and me. Their main objective is to keep their job. The truth is, they do not have much interest in your loan. They would just like it to close, so they can get a bonus. But if it doesn't close, they will still get their paycheck. So don't get mad at the underwriter.

Instead, make underwriters your friend. They get yelled at enough by other brokers. If you show them some kindness, they will return the favor by getting your loans through underwriting faster.

The process of underwriting is sometimes the longest part of the loan. Lenders try to get loans through underwriting in 2-3 business days. But when they are very busy, it can take over 9. So if your lock is about the expire and your loan is sitting in underwriting, it is in your best interest to be on good terms with the underwriters, who can push your file to the head of the line and save your commission in the process.

What Is An Appraiser?

The appraiser tells you the value of the property. Almost all loans need an appraisal. The appraiser is also someone you should be good friends with, since he is the one who determines how much your borrowers can borrow.

The appraisal is an art, not a science. Send 10 appraisers to the same house and all of them will give you different values. They might be in the same ballpark, but they will all be different.

So if you find a "liberal" appraiser, be sure to keep him happy. For example, you are doing a refinance for a couple who need to take out $20,000 of equity from their house or they won't do the loan. Their balance is $50,000 and your lender will only lend up to 80% of the value. Closing costs can be assumed to be $4000. The appraisal comes in at $90,000. You have a problem, because you need the house to be worth $92,500 in order for the borrower to get 20K out. If you are on good terms with your appraiser, you can suggest that you need a value of at least $92,500. And if he likes you, he will do his best to justify an appraisal of $92,500.

WHERE DO I GET THE CREDIT REPORTS?

Your company should have an account set up with a local credit reseller. You get all your credit reports from this company. And you can usually do it by computer. No need to talk to anyone or fax anything. Just enter in the data of the borrowers and their credit report will print on your printer.

Understanding the report will come with time and you can find out exactly how to do so in *Residential Loan Origination Made Easy*. (Ordering info is available at the back of the book.)

The most important thing to notice is the credit score. The higher the score, the better the credit and the better the chances of the borrower getting a loan. If the score is 620 or above, it qualifies as a conforming loan. Under 620 makes it sub-prime.

To learn how easy it is to raise someone's credit scores read the book, *How To Make Your Credit Sparkle* which is also available at our website. **http://www.creditsparkle.com**

WHAT DOES THE TITLE COMPANY DO?

The title company does many things. B   imary role is to make sure that the title on the ho This means that no one besides the seller ownership of the property. If everything i issue Title Insurance, which protects the there is ever any problem with the title

Without clear title, the lender will not lend the money and the loan will not close. The title company also works as an escrow company and keeps all the funds until closing. When all the paperwork is complete, the lender wires the money into the title company's account. The title company will then prepare all the closing documents, get everyone's signatures and distribute all the checks.

A real estate closing attorney can also serve the same function as a title company. It really depends in which state you live in if you use, title companies or escrow companies, or closing attorneys.

The fees charged by the title company are passed on to the buyers and sellers. In the sales contract, it specifies who will pay for the title charges.

CHAPTER 9

How Do People Choose Their Broker?

Over 65% of Americans use mortgage brokers. Brokers provide consumers with:

- Choice
- Convenience
- Expertise

The consumer receives an expert mentor through the complex mortgage-lending process. The broker offers the consumer extensive choices and access to affordable home loans while balancing the consumer's financial interests and goals.

So the question really is, "Why wouldn't someone use a mortgage broker?"

WHAT ABOUT THE COMPETITION?

There are a ton of mortgage companies in every city. They seem to be everywhere. So I cannot say that there is not a lot of competition. There is. But it doesn't matter. You could not do all the loans in your town by yourself anyway. There is enough business to go around. Over $2 trillion in loans are originated every year. That is a lot of money.

If you provide good customer service, are knowledgeable about your loan products, take the time to care about your prospects and their needs, you will have more business than you can handle.

The National Association of Realtors does yearly surveys of homebuyers and some of the results are listed below. These are for the 2003 survey.

91% of all homebuyers obtained a mortgage for their home purchase.

Why do they choose their mortgage lender? These were their reasons:

14% price
16% reputation
14% they had used the lender before
36% the lender was recommended by their agent
13% the lender recommended by family or friends.

Only 56% of homebuyers would definitely use their mortgage lender again. That shows that almost half the mortgage companies are not doing their job properly. This is very good news for those companies that really do a great job of customer satisfaction.

On average, homebuyers had a Loan-To-Value ratio of 84%. That means that on average people got loans of 84% of the value of the house.

48% of all buyers only went to one mortgage company.

When did they get a pre-approval?

38% before looking for a house
30% while searching for a house
28% after they found a house
5% never. They were not pre-approved.

Where did buyers find out about lenders?

41% from their agent
32% from the Internet
28% from friends/family
26% from going to different lenders
20% from newspapers
16% from telephone
6% from direct mail
5% from TV commercials.

So what do these numbers tell us?

1. Referrals are very important. Referrals from Realtors, friends, and family make up a large percentage of the reason why people choose a mortgage company.

2. Since a large number of people only visit one mortgage company, the risk of competition is not as high as one would think.

3. Price is not that big a deal when choosing a lender.

4. Traditional advertising (radio, TV, newspaper) is not as effective as word-of-mouth advertising. And it is a lot more expensive!

CHAPTER 10

The Keys to Success as a Mortgage Broker

Charles Schwab once said, "A man, to carry on a successful business, must have imagination. He must see things as in a vision, a dream of the whole thing." His words are true for both men and women who want to start in the mortgage brokerage business. Imagination is a major requirement.

WHAT WILL YOU NEED TO BE A SUCCESSFUL MORTGAGE BROKER?

Certainly you'll need your own special knowledge, skills, talent, some money, and a lot of time. But just as necessary is a personal desire to help others. This is important if you are an employee and is vital if you are an owner.

As a consumer, you can easily read the attitude of people who serve you. You know when someone is helping you because it is their job or because they enjoy doing their job. And clients usually respond by supporting and recommending those who help us solve our problems and make us feel important. They appreciate our business, and they get it.

Before you decide whether mortgage brokerage is for you, you must know who you are. What do you feel most comfortable doing? Under what conditions do you enjoy working with people? Under what conditions do you prefer to avoid people? What are your personal goals? What are your financial goals? How much risk do you feel comfortable taking? Most important, is financing a good fit in your life or would it cause more problems than it cures? Self-analysis can be difficult, but it is the only way of ensuring that this is what will bring you the results you want in life.

Maybe by this stage in your life you've developed a list of personal goals for the next year, five years, and beyond. Most people have not. It is not mandatory that you develop a long list of your life goals before you start in this business, but it will increase your chances of personal and financial success. You can begin by answering these questions for yourself:

- What is it you want from your life?
- Do you have specific goals?
- What plans do you have for the next year of your life?
- Is there anything that people often complement you about?
- Is there some work or task you would do even if you were not paid?
- Is there some opportunity that strikes you as worthwhile?

PERSONAL VALUES

Values are tools that will take you toward your personal goals. Values are standards and qualities that you have established to help you make daily decisions. Those people who succeed in business have some common personal knowledge. Let's look at those values together to determine your strength in opportunities.

Self-awareness. The process of starting and operating a business is difficult. It will work if you constantly test yourself, maintaining what works and changing what doesn't. But that's what many people love about being a business owner, the endless challenges. It makes them aware of their characteristics and requires that they continue to grow.

Hard work. Being an independent businessman means that you get to select which 12 hours of the day you are going to work. Just kidding. But don't expect to work just a 40-hour week at least at first and you won't be disappointed.

Discipline. Discipline is the power behind hard work. You can know exactly what needs to be done and still not do it. Self-discipline forces you to act. Having goals that are meaningful to you will increase your self-discipline.

Independence. Great business owners often make poor employees. They are too independent. They cannot, however, be stubborn. Business owners must maintain a balance between independence and open-mindedness to succeed.

Self-confidence. It takes a lot of nerve to start a business. It takes a lot more to make it successful. But nerve or self-confidence is not equal. It is a belief in your unique skills founded on past success. You know you can successfully operate as a mortgage broker because you have the skills to do so, not just the desire.

Adaptability. Life is chaos. No matter how much we plan, people and events change. Products change. Markets change. We change. A successful business owner must adapt to these changes. It's a hassle sometimes. But remember, without change, life becomes very dull.

Judgment. To succeed in business, you must make good decisions every day. Wisdom requires knowledge. You must be able to gather complete and accurate facts in order to make the best decision you can from those facts. You will not be right every time, but you will be right most of the time. This is good judgment.

Stress tolerance. Stress has been defined as "the confusion created when your mind overrides your body's basic desire to club someone who desperately deserves it." Humor can help reduce stress. Stress is a part of every day life, especially in business. Learning to live with stress without taking it personally can help you succeed in business.

Need to achieve. Success is the achievement of something you set out to do. It may be the completion of a project, or the start of a business, or the learning of a new skill. This need is a driving force within successful business owners that helps give them the energy to reach their goal.

About Your Financial Goals

As much as you may love helping people, you must also have financial goals. Without a fair salary and profit, you won't be able to help people get a loan.

What is an appropriate financial goal for you? If your business goal is to open your own office within three years, your financial goal must be one that will fund such an ambitious goal. If your business takes off and is successful, and you want to then sell it in 10 years and retire, your financial goals must match what you expect your selling price of your business will be. If your business goal is to make a salary as well as a fair return on your investment, you must first determine what a good salary and return are to you.

One successful mortgage broker established a financial goal of developing annual sales of $200,000 within three years in order to take on a partner who could offer other financial services. He then wanted to spend two more years developing the single location before selling the business to the partner for enough to pay off his home mortgage and do some traveling. His goals were specific and attainable.

Your Risk Tolerance

Business is legalized gambling. When you start any business you're gambling that you'll succeed. How much does this risk bother you? Are you risk tolerant?

You must determine your own risk tolerance and that of those with whom you share your life. If you're ready to take the plunge, but your spouse would rather not, find a mutually acceptable level of risk before starting your business. Or else you may find, as do many people have that you traded an invaluable relationship for a replaceable business.

Generating Business

Mortgage brokerage is a people business. The more people you know, the more loans you have the opportunity to do. It has been estimated that each person alive knows about 1000 other people. Sounds like a large number, but it has been scientifically studied.

Out of all the people you know, I am sure there are many that you wouldn't want to work with, and some that wouldn't work with you, for whatever reason.

So the average person's sphere of influence (the group of known people you can market to) is much less than 1000. It's closer to about 300. Given that at least 10% of the population moves every year, that gives the average mortgage broker a shot at 30 loans a year without doing any other marketing.

But in the beginning you will not have such a large sphere of influence. So while you build your own, you can use other peoples' spheres. There are many other professionals that also use the sphere of influence marketing concept: Realtors, insurance agents, financial planners, and anyone else who has a customer list.

The easiest way to increase your sales and your sphere is to convince one of these business owners to sell you to their customers. They can write a testimonial saying how wonderful you are and then mail it to their customers.

Or you can just get their names, or even pay for the names and addresses. Big companies do this all the time. You might not believe this, but there are lists available on any topic you could think of. For example, you can get a list of subscribers for every magazine in the country. You can get a list of people that buy Dean Martin videos. You can get a list of people who own houses worth over $1 million, with no mortgage and who own another house in Hawaii. The lists are endless.

My point is, while you should do your best to build your own list, you can in the meantime use someone else's to market to. And if you can get the list owner to recommend you, your marketing will be a lot more effective.

Let me prove it to you. Now that you have bought this book, you are on my list. Let's say that one day, you get two letters in the mail. One is from me saying that Joe's Mortgage Licensing School is the best school I have seen and that you should check it out. The other letter is from a company called Mary's Licensing School saying how good they are.

Which one sound's better? If you have enjoyed this book and feel that I know what I am talking about, then you will probably choose Joe's school.

This is the power of the endorsement. I endorsed Joe's school and my endorsement to my own list will carry a lot of weight, especially since my list already knows and trusts me.

The same is true for you. As people begin to know your work and trust you, you will come to know the same power of endorsement.

How Do I Get Clients?

There are a zillion different ways to get customers and clients. In fact, my company has several different manuals and systems that show brokers how to get customers.

You can:
- go after the homebuyer market.
- go after the refinance market
- go after the people about to be foreclosed on market.
- broker loans for investors.
- broker loans for businesses
- factor account receivables.
- buy and sell notes and mortgages.
- do second mortgages.

- focus on apartment complexes or shopping centers.
- do construction loans
- do church financing
- do home equity loans
- do FHA or VA loans
- do sub-prime loans
- do SBA loans
- do business start-up or machinery acquisition loans
- focus on first-time homebuyers
- focus on homebuyers in bankruptcy

and the list goes on and on

It is not advisable for you to try to do everything. Even though that is what a lot of brokers do. Whenever someone asks them about a particular loan, whether it be for a personal residence or a commercial loan, they will say that they can do it. And then try to find out how.

The most successful brokers, find a niche they feel comfortable with, then dominate that niche. If someone in your town is regarded as the expert in financing homes over $1 million, then the people buying these homes, the builders building them, and the Realtors selling them will all come to this broker so that the deal goes through.

After you are done with your initial training, you should be focused on generating business for the rest of your career. There are many different ways to do this.

For example, working with only one Realtor who refers you one loan a month can put over $40,000 in your pocket per year. And you can work with as many Realtors as you want. But getting them to work with you is the hard part. Every loan officer in town goes after Realtors.

If you set yourself apart from the others, you ' better chance.

If you would like more information on exactly how. to get Realtors to want to work with you, visit: **www. marketingtorealtors.com**.

You also need to generate referrals from your past clients, friends, and family. But there are good ways to ask for business and bad ways to ask.

At our website: **www.mortgagebrokertraining.com** one of our newest products is a marketing system that shows you

- why referrals are the easiest and cheapest way to get loans
- how to turn each clients into a walking, talking billboard for your business
- how to handle each referral so it turns into multiple loans

Having a website is also a good way to generate customers.

Direct mail and direct marketing can work wonders as well, if you do it right. But it is not as easy as it first appears.

Generating loans is the hardest part of the business. That's why we get paid the big bucks.

As you continue in this industry, make a serious effort to learn as much about marketing as you can. Anything you see that you consider good marketing can be adapted and used in the mortgage arena.

At the back of this book, are descriptions of a few of the items we have available to help brokers generate as many loans as possible.

CHAPTER **11**

Mortgage Banking

Mortgage banking is similar to mortgage brokerage, except that you are working for the lender.

In this chapter, we will go over some aspects of mortgage baking, in case you decide to go that route. Most positions at a mortgage bank are fixed-paycheck jobs. So if the thought of only working on commission scares you, but you still want to work in finance, this might be the way to go.

WHAT EXACTLY IS MORTGAGE BANKING?

The mortgage lending industry makes, sells and services mortgages secured by residential, multi-family and commercial real estate. The mortgage lending process is a complex series of interrelated activities, which offers you a number of different job opportunities. To help you better identify the best match for your interests and abilities, let's first review the various activities associated with mortgage lending.

• **Origination** is the creation of mortgage applications. Loan originators (loan officers and brokers) are the sales force in the real estate finance industry. Loan officers do the job of mortgage brokers for the lender. Whether a loan officer or a broker, the loan originator initiates the origination process by locating borrowers and making loan applications.

- **Processing** is the collection of documentation and verifications to support information provided on the loan application. Among the documents obtained by the processor are the appraisal, which confirms the value of the mortgaged property, and a credit report, which discloses the borrower's credit history.

- **Underwriting** is the evaluation of loan documentation to approve or deny the loan. During the evaluation process, the underwriter analyzes whether the loan represents an acceptable risk to the lender. An important aspect of the evaluation process is determining whether the loan meets the requirements that make it saleable to investors in the secondary mortgage market.

- **Closing** is the consummation of the loan transaction. The closing process involves the delivery of a deed, the signing of the note, and the disbursement of loan funds.

- **Warehousing** is the method by which most mortgage bankers fund the loans at closing. Warehousing involve short-term borrowing of funds from warehouse banks using permanent mortgage loans as collateral. The money borrowed from this line of credit is used to produce mortgage loans. Once the loans are sold to an investor on the secondary market, the mortgage banker replenishes the warehouse line, enabling it to use the funds to create more loans.

- **Shipping and delivery** is the packaging of closed loan files for delivery to an investor. This consummates the loan sale and all activities associated with "loan production."

- **Secondary marketing** is the sale of closed loans to investors, the development and pricing of loan programs, and the management of the risk associated with funding mortgages. Normally, the sale to investors is arranged simultaneously with the origination of loans. Commitments are used to secure the future sale of loans and protect against interest rate changes that may occur between the dates of origination and sale.

- **Loan administration (servicing)** is the collection, recordation and remittance of monthly mortgage payments to investors. Servicing also includes the maintenance of escrows to protect the property securing each loan.

CHAPTER 12

Commercial Loans

Commercial lending involves the same real estate issues as residential lending, including borrower credit, underwriting, loan documentation, loan appraisal, loan sale, loan hedging and loan administration. But the business aspects of commercial properties makes commercial lending more complicated. And it requires professionals with a slightly different skill set.

Commercial real estate is more than just the real estate; it also includes leasing of commercial real estate -- houses, offices, warehouses, industrial sites, hotels, stores, apartment complexes, etc.

Even when buying and selling is involved, commercial real estate is ultimately focused on rent. Rent is the driving force of any commercial real estate project, because it provides the cash flow that supports the commercial real estate venture.

WHAT SKILLS DO I NEED?

Commercial mortgage lenders require more business education and analytical skills than do the residential lenders. Commercial lenders should also be well-versed in spreadsheets, databases, graphical analysis and geographic information systems.

How Much Can I Make?

Commercial loan officers work on a 100% commission. Commercial loan officers with 1 to 3 years of experience earn between $48,000 and $64,750. With over 3 years of experience, commercial loan officers could make between $66,000 and $95,250 (Source: Department of Labor, Occupational Outlook Handbook).

CHAPTER 13

The Future of the Business

The future of the industry looks very bright indeed.

Homeownership is something that will never go out of style.

Everyone is telling people to own their own homes -- the government, financial planners, investment gurus, and everybody in between.

Every few years, interest rates drop and there is a refinance boom. The year of 2003 was such a time. Everyone that owned a house wanted to refinance. And some people even did it twice as rates kept dropping.

While we don't see such booms every year, new housing continues to be strong and with the government's support, homeowner initiatives will always be around.

In fact, the following HUD press release shows how the government will make it much easier for people to buy homes and thus increase our market.

BUSH ADMINISTRATION ANNOUNCES NEW HUD "ZERO DOWN PAYMENT" MORTGAGE

INITIATIVE AIMED AT REMOVING MAJOR BARRIER TO HOMEOWNERSHIP

Las Vegas—As part of President Bush's ongoing effort to help American families achieve the dream of homeownership, Federal Housing Commissioner John C. Weicher today announced that HUD is proposing to offer a "zero down payment" mortgage, the most significant initiative by the Federal Housing Administration in over a decade. This action would help remove the greatest barrier facing first-time homebuyers - the lack of funds for a down payment on a mortgage.

Speaking at the National Association of Home Builders' annual convention, Commissioner Weicher indicated that the proposal, part of HUD's Fiscal Year 2005 budget request, would eliminate the statutory requirement of a minimum three percent down payment for FHA-insured single-family mortgages for first-time homebuyers.

"Offering FHA mortgages with no down payment will unlock the door to homeownership for hundreds of thousands of American families, particularly minorities," said HUD's Acting Secretary Alphonso Jackson. "President Bush has pledged to create 5.5 million new minority homeowners this decade, and this historic initiative will help meet this goal."

Preliminary projections indicate that the new FHA mortgage product would generate about 150,000 homebuyers in the first year alone.

"This initiative would not only address a major hurdle to homeownership and allow many renters to afford their own home, it would help these families build wealth and become true stakeholders in their communities," said Commissioner Weicher. "In addition, it would help spur the production of new housing in this country."

For those that choose to participate in the Zero Down Payment program, HUD would charge a modestly higher insurance premium, which would be phased down over several years, and would also require families to undergo pre-purchase housing counseling.

HUD is the nation's housing agency committed to increasing homeownership, particularly among minorities; creating affordable housing opportunities for low-income Americans; and supporting the homeless, elderly, people with disabilities and people living with AIDS. The Department also promotes economic and community development as well as enforces the nation's fair housing laws. More information about HUD and its programs is available on the Internet at http://www.hud.gov/ and espanol.hud.gov.

	Previous	**Current**
The homeownership rate in the third quarter 2003 (68.4 percent) was higher than the revised third quarter 2002 rate (68.0 percent). The homeownership rate in the West was higher than one year ago, while rates in the Northeast, Midwest, and South remained statistically unchanged.	68.0 percent 3rd Qtr. 2002	68.4 percent 3rd Qtr. 2003

Source: U.S. Census Bureau as of October 28, 2003.

CHAPTER **14**

Training Sources

SMALL BUSINESS ADMINISTRATION RESOURCES

Founded more than 45 years ago, the US Small Business Administration, or SBA, has offices in 100 cities across the United States and the character to help small businesses start and grow. The SBA offers counseling, booklets on business topics, and administers a small-business loan guarantee program.

[To find your area's SBA office, check the white pages and telephone books in your region under "United States Government, Small Business Administration."]

The SBA offers numerous publications, services, and videos for starting and managing small businesses. Publications are available on products, ideas, inventions, financial management, management and planning, marketing, crime prevention, personal management, and other topics.

[The booklets can be purchased for one or two dollars each at SBA offices or from SBA publications, P.O. Box 30, Denver, c/o 80201. Ask first for SBA form 115 a, the small-business directory, that lists available publication and includes an order form.]

The Service Corps of Retired Executives is a national nonprofit association with the goal of helping small businesses. SCORE is sponsored by the SBA and the local office is usually in or near that of the local SBA office. SCORE members, retired men and women, and those still active in their own business, donate their time and experience to countless individuals regarding small-business issues.

TAX INFORMATION RESOURCES

The US Treasury Department Internal Revenue Service offers numerous small-business tax education program videos through their regional offices. Topics include depreciation, business use of your home, employment taxes, excise taxes, starting a business, partnership, self-employed retirement plans, Subchapter S corporations, and federal tax deposits.

If you're considering using a portion of your home as a business office, request publication 587 from the Internal Revenue Service. It's free and will help you determine if your business qualifies for this option.

What business expenses are deductible? There's a long list. The best answers are found in the free publication offered by the IRS, business expenses publication 535.

You can get all these resources play the contacting the IRS directly or visiting their web site at **www.irs.gov**

WHAT IS CONTINUING EDUCATION?

Continuing education is a necessary part of the business. And with good reason. There are so many changes the industry goes through every year that, unless you constantly educate yourself, you will be lost in the dust.

Most states with licenses also require that brokers spend a set amount of hours in classes every year. If you do not, you lose your license. Again, this is a good thing. If the continuing education requirement pertains to you, do not look at it as a chore. Instead, try to get the most out of it. There are so many things to know, that no one can know everything. And the more you learn, the more professional you can be and the more people you can help.

MORTGAGE RESOURCES

The mortgage industry though highly regulated does not have that many sources for education and training. But this is changing. As more people come into the business, more schools and training programs are being established. Some are better than others.

My company, Kamrock Publishing, in partnership with MoneyTree Mortgage, is dedicated to helping mortgage professionals achieve all they desire. To do so, we have create our website www.mortgagebrokertraining.com with you in mind.

Our products include mortgage training manuals, credit repair manuals, marketing manuals, and other training products

There are also a few magazines dedicated to the mortgage industry. If you are a member of your local association of mortgage brokers, you will receive their monthly magazine as well as NAMB's magazine called Broker.

sources:

ews.com

...ansguide.com

www.mortgagemag.com

In all these publications you will find advertisements for lenders, net branches, software vendors, credit report resellers, and any other vendor looking to sell to mortgage people.

CHAPTER 15

Other Questions

How Do I Motivate Myself?

Motivation is key to success in this business. As a commissioned mortgage broker you are your own boss. You control what you do with your time. It is very easy to spend an hour every day reading the newspaper instead of looking for new business.

There are certain things you need to do. Prospecting is one of these things. Without new loans, you will have no future income. And getting new loans is what you are paid to do.

If you have never been in total control of your time before, you might find that you do not have the discipline to work effectively.

But do not despair. It happens to all of us. There are many times where I spend too much time reading the news on the internet instead of doing what I should be doing.

The way to overcome this is to have focus. Goofing off is OK, if you get done everything that needs to be done.

Ask yourself the following questions:

- Why am I working?
- What will I do with my extra money?
- What is it that I want more than anything else?
- How do I reach my goals?
- What are my goals?

These are hard questions. And if you have never asked yourself these questions before, you need to sit down and determine your answers. What you need to come up with is the thing that keeps you going. It will help motivate you when things get rough. I cannot lie to you and say that mortgage brokerage is an easy business. It is not. It is like everything else, if you put in the time needed you will succeed. But it will not be overnight and it will not be easy.

So when times get tough, you need to keep focused on the big goals, your priorities, and your dreams. Without these, it is very easy to fall victim to the temptation to quit.

Many mortgage brokers do quit. They find that they cannot handle the freedom. They cannot handle not having someone telling them what to do all the time.

Being a mortgage broker is not a 9-5 job—at least not until you become successful. It is a 7-day-a-week job. If you have no loans and you get a hot lead, but the borrower can only meet you on Sunday, you will meet him on Sunday.

After you start doing well, you will not have to go running after borrowers. They will come after you. If you provide great service, the word will spread. And borrowers will go out of their way to work with you. But it won't happen in the beginning.

Sure, you do not have to wake up until noon, then can go home at 2:00 in the afternoon. And no one is going to say anything to you if you act that way. But when it comes time to pay the bills, you won't have any excuses.

ARE MORTGAGES A SEASONAL BUSINESS?

Mortgages are needed all the time. People move all the time. So mortgage brokerage is not a seasonal business in the traditional sense.

There are certain months that are better than others. The summer months are the busiest. Families with kids prefer to move in the summer so the kids do not have to miss school. December is a very slow month. With the holidays around the corner, very few people think about buying a new house in December.

Refinancing is another ball game completely. People refinance when rates go down. They want to take advantage of the new lower interest rates before they go back up. The year of 2003 was great for refinances. The whole year was very hot. Rates were at their lowest levels in years. And people took advantage of it.

Mortgage brokers were super busy refinancing everybody. Even people who had bought a house a year earlier were refinancing. Some people refinanced more than once in 2003. It was crazy. These times are called Refinance Booms. It is easy money for lenders and brokers. And like all good things, these times come to an end. By December 2003, unless they lived under a rock, everyone who was going to refinance had refinanced. So the boom dried up.

On the other hand, when rates are high, times are tough for mortgage brokers. In the 1980's, when rates were up to 16-17% very few people bought houses. And no one refinanced. Hopefully, rates will not go up that much again for a long time.

Overall, the Federal Reserve has done a great job in the last two decades keeping interest rates low. The economy has been good and real estate continues to appreciate.

Owning a home is still the American Dream. People will always want to buy houses. And the government makes it advantageous to buy a house instead of renting. All these factors show that mortgage brokers are not going anywhere. They will be around for a long time.

How Do I Hide My Inexperience?

Borrowers typically do not ask you how long you have been in the business. But if they find out that you are new, they may be turned off.

At first, you should solicit business from your family and friends. Since they know you, they will know that you just got into the business. But they shouldn't mind, especially when you assure them that a senior loan officer in your firm will oversee everything you are doing to make sure it goes smoothly.

The best way to seem experienced is to act experienced. Know the jargon. Know the paperwork. Know the loan programs that are most commonly used in your office. Study the business until you can talk in mortgage fluently.

It will not take long. After just 2-3 loans you will know what to expect in most situations. After more loans it will become second nature to you.

If you have an office, decorate it with trophies and certificates. It doesn't matter what they are for. They are there just to show the borrowers that you are someone that has been recognized as being something special. They probably won't even take the time to see what the awards are for. But the awards being there will go along way in making them feel at ease with their loan in your hands.

Remember, that a mortgage is the largest debt most people have. And their home is considered their most valuable asset.

WHY BUYING A HOME IS A GOOD IDEA

• The Best Investment

As a general rule, homes appreciate about four or five percent a year. Some years will be more, some less. The figure will vary from neighborhood to neighborhood, and region to region.

Five percent may not seem like that much at first. Stocks (at times) appreciate much more, and you could easily earn over the same return with a very safe investment in treasury bills or bonds.

But take a second look...

Presumably, if you bought a $200,000 house, you did not pay cash. You got a mortgage, too. Suppose you put as much as twenty percent down – that would be an investment of $40,000.

At an appreciation rate of 5% annually, a $200,000 home would increase in value $10,000 during the first year. That means you earned $10,000 with an investment of $40,000. Your annual "return on investment" would be a whopping twenty-five percent.

Of course, you are making mortgage payments and paying property taxes, along with a couple of other costs. However, since the interest on your mortgage and your property taxes are both tax deductible, the government is essentially subsidizing your home purchase.

Your rate of return when buying a home is higher than most any other investment you could make.

- **Income Tax Savings**

Because of income tax deductions, the government is subsidizing your purchase of a home. All of the interest and property taxes you pay in a given year can be deducted from your gross income to reduce your taxable income.

For example, assume your initial loan balance is $150,000 with an interest rate of eight percent. During the first year you would pay $9969.27 in interest. If your first payment is January 1st, your taxable income would be almost $10,000 less – due to the IRS interest rate deduction.

Property taxes are deductible, too. Whatever property taxes you pay in a given year may also be deducted from your gross income, lowering your tax obligation.

- **Stable Monthly Housing Costs**

When you rent a place to live, you can certainly expect your rent to increase each year—or even more often. If you get a fixed rate mortgage when you buy a home, you have the same monthly payment amount for thirty years. Even if you get an adjustable rate mortgage, your payment will stay within a certain range for the entire life of the mortgage—and interest rates aren't as volatile now as they were in the late Seventies and early Eighties.

Imagine how much rent might be ten, fifteen, or even thirty years from now? Which makes more sense?

FORCED SAVINGS

Some people are just lousy at saving money. A house is an automatic savings account. You accumulate savings in two ways. Every month, a portion of your payment goes toward the principal. Admittedly, in the early years of the mortgage, this is not much. Over time, however, it accelerates.

Second, your home appreciates. Average appreciation on a home is approximately five percent, though it will vary from year to year, and in some years may even depreciate.. Over time, history has shown that owning a home is one of the very best financial investments.

- **Freedom & Individualism**

When you rent, you are normally limited on what you can do to improve your home. You have to get permission to make certain types of improvements. Nor does it make sense to spend thousand of dollars painting, putting in carpet, tile or window coverings when the main person who benefits is the landlord and not you.

Since your landlord wants to keep his expenses to a minimum, he or she will probably not be spending much to improve the place either.

When you own a home, however, you can do pretty much whatever you want. You get the benefits of any improvements you make, plus you get to live in an environment you have created, not some faceless landlord.

- **More Space**

Both indoors and outdoors, you will probably have more space if you own your own home. Even moving to a condominium from an apartment, you are likely to find you have much more room available – your own laundry and storage area, and bigger rooms. Apartment complexes are more interested in creating the maximum number of income-producing units than they are in creating space for each of the tenants.

If you are moving to a home for the first time, you are going to be very pleased with all the new space you have available. You may have to even buy more "stuff."

CHAPTER 16

Dos and Don'ts

Some final words of advice to you.

IF YOU HAVEN'T DECIDED TO BECOME A BROKER YET:

DO think it over. Take a few days to weigh the pros and cons explained in this book. Talk to someone in the business and find out what they think about it.

DO NOT make a rush decision. Becoming successful will take some time. Making a career move is not something you decide to do over lunch.

DO read this book over again. Make sure you understand what will be required of you.

DO NOT make this decision without consulting your spouse or family. Sacrifices will have to be made by you and your family as well. So don't leave them out.

IF YOU HAVE DECIDED TO BECOME A MORTGAGE BROKER:

DO start right away. Don't waste time. Take action right away.

DO NOT worry if you made the right choice. Listen to your gut, your inner voice, your soul. It will never lead you astray.

DO read everything you can. Start reading about mortgage brokers right away.

DO NOT neglect your training.

DO visit mortgage lenders in your area. Pose as a potential borrower. Discover what they offer. See how they present the disclosures. Determine which approach you like best. Model yours after the one you choose.

DO NOT start working at the first company you come to. Research several companies before you decide.

DO read this book over. And this time, take notes.

DO make a list of everyone you know. Tell them of your decision, so you can ask them for business.

DO set clear goals. Make sure you know why you are choosing this profession.

DO have fun.

DO rely on me. Remember that my company and I are here to make your transition easy and to help you be as successful as possible.

We want to help you achieve everything you dream of. Visit our site: www.mortgagebrokertraining.com regularly and subscribe to the free newsletter to keep up-to-date on happenings in the marketplace.

In order to provide a balanced view of the business, we asked a number of our mortgage broker customers to answer a few questions for us relating to the business. These are presented in the next chapter.

CHAPTER 17

Interviews

All the responses are from people active in the business. We tried to get as broad a mix as possible. We have interviews of company owners, branch managers, loan officers, and consultants. Some are very new (only a few months in the business), and some have been around for decades.

Every interview offers something. I have taken the liberty to highlight what I though were the most important points made in each interview. And in some I have added my own comments before the interview.

Please note: The opinions given in the interviews are those of the person interviewed. They are not necessarily the opinions of the author or the publisher. The answers given are meant to be guidelines and not specific advice. Please carefully weigh all options before following any advice given to you.

Also, an answer from one interviewee might contradict an answer from another. That is why we interviewed so many; To give you a complete feel of the business from insiders. Hopefully, by using this book you will be able to avoid the frustrations our panel endured.

Name: Jim Rainey
Title: Owner
Organization: RainWalk Financial Center
Place: Colorado Springs, CO
Email: rainwalkfin@aol.com

How long have you been in the mortgage brokerage business?
Three years

What is your yearly loan volume?
$8-10M

What do you like best about your job?
Helping people achieve the American dream of home-ownership

What do you like least about your job?
Not being able to get a truly deserving couple financed in a timely manner

What advice would you give a person starting today?
Make your focus helping people and not just making money. If you truly help people, the money will come.

Knowing what you know now, what would you have done differently in your mortgage career?
Learned much more about lead generation resources early on

Please describe your job description.
Owner/Broker/Processor

What one tool would you say is essential to a newcomer in the business?
Establishing realtor and banker referral sources

Is there any other advice you would give?
Despite temptations to the contrary, maintain your integrity above reproach at all times and in all of your dealings with your clients, referral sources, lenders, and your colleagues.

Name: Drew Miranda
Title: Branch Manager
Organization: Icon Financial Group
Email: dmiranda@iconfinancial.com

How long have you been in the mortgage brokerage business?
12 years

What is your yearly loan volume?
Greater than $20 million

What do you like best about your job?
The ability to solve problems using creative funding sources and techniques

What do you like least about your job?

Pushy realtors who truly don't understand what it takes to get some people approved.

What advice would you give a person starting today?
Once you're in the business there are plenty of people to help resolve problems and make the loan fund, but focus on marketing yourself from day one, there is no one to teach you that and you can take that anywhere you go.

Knowing what you know now, what would you have done differently in your mortgage career?
Invested more time in developing systems to automate the processes and generate more leads from my marketing efforts.

Please describe your job description
Responsible for the recruiting, and retainment of quality loan originators as well as providing them with the marketing systems the need to be successful.

What one tool would you say is essential to a newcomer in the business?
A solid marketing system must be in place; and you can't always depend on most companies to provide it

Is there any other advice you would give?
Life is to short to work with people you don't enjoy working with, in an environment that you don't feel comfortable in, doing something you don't truly enjoy; and it will show in your performance.

Name: Robert Dawson, CRMS
Title: Vice President/Operations Manager
Organization: Buckeye Mortgage Group, Inc
Address: Akron, Ohio
Email: jacred22@aol.com

How long have you been in the mortgage brokerage business?
Nine years

What is your yearly loan volume?
$25-30 million

What do you like best about your job?
Helping first time homebuyers realize the dream of home ownership. Especially the ones that don't think they can buy a home. The look in their eyes on closing day makes it all worthwhile.

What do you like least about your job?
The hours. I work an average of 65-70 hours per week. Also, not everyone that I deal with moves as quickly as I like to. That gets frustrating

What advice would you give a person starting today?
Find a good company and be a loan officer. That is where the money is, not in ownership. Develop Realtor sources and concentrate on purchase business. Treat people fairly and always tell the truth, even if its bad news. Don't be greedy and always remember where you came from

Knowing what you know now, what would you have done differently in your mortgage career?
Remained a loan officer instead of opening my own shop. Now I have the headaches of 30 loan officers, along with my own. Make 50-60% somewhere and close 30-40k per month. You do the math. It's a great living.

Please describe your job description.
I run the day to day operations and am also the top producer in my company.

Is there any other advice you would give?
Work hard. Stay focused. And never get too high or too low.

This interview is of a wholesale account representative, not a mortgage broker. This man works for a lender to fund loans sent to him by mortgage brokers.

Name: Darrin L. Haug
Title: Northern California Top Account Executive
Organization: Planet Financial Services
Email: dar2exl@sbcglobal.net

How long have you been in the mortgage brokerage business?
Three years

What is your yearly loan volume?
$3-5+ million per month

What do you like best about your job?
The challenge, the pressure to perform, the freedom and that I have a direct hand in helping people achieve there dreams of home ownership

What do you like least about your job?
Come end month it gets a bit crazy as all brokers tend to wait until then. Probably more from fall-out at other lenders more than just procrastination

What advice would you give a person starting today?
Know your guidelines and programs. Product knowledge is such a key. Be accountable, be available.

Knowing what you know now, what would you have done differently in your mortgage career?
Started sooner

Please describe your job description.
Wholesale Account Executive for a direct lender, purchasing residential loan packages

What one tool would you say is essential to a newcomer in the business?
Knowledge

Is there any other advice you would give?
Just work smart, work long hours and know your products and guidelines better than everyone else.

Name: Patsy Taylor
Title: Loan Originator
Organization: World Leadership Group
Email: pattaylor@wlgdirect.com

How long have you been in the mortgage brokerage business?
Six months

What do you like best about your job?
Helping clients who are in the refinance market harness the power of their mortgage. I am excited about new home purchasers because we educate these clients on what type of home loan programs to shop for.

What do you like least about your job?
It is very time consuming.

What advice would you give a person starting today?
Get excited. Stay focused and put God first, family second and you will never be last!!

Knowing what you know now, what would you have done differently in your mortgage career?
I would have started a lot sooner than I did.

Please describe your job description.
My job title is that of Loan originator. It is my responsibility to create my own clientele. I help a potential client find the best loan program to fit their needs. When that loan is found I then forward it to the loan processor. This can be done electronically via the internet.

What one tool would you say is essential to a newcomer in the business?
A desk or laptop computer!!

Is there any other advice you would give?
Yes. I would hope that people understand the importance of getting a big 30 year mortgage and never pay it off. Take advantage of the interest only and cash flow programs. Get into a property with less money down, and invest the difference.

Name: Robert McAvoy
Title: Branch Manager
Organization: MortgageAll Express
Address: Hampstead, NH
Email: rwmcavoy@juno.com

How long have you been in the mortgage brokerage business?
Six years

What do you like best about your job?
I always get a nice feeling in helping buyers obtain financing for their first home. Also being able to help people refinance so they can either start a business, do home improvements, help their children pay for college, and other emergencies makes you feel your job is important.

What do you like least about your job?
Not being able to help people because they have such damaged credit and they are not willing to take your advice on how they can improve it enough to be able to help them. Most of these people have such a bad attitude and feel the world owes them a living.

What advice would you give a person starting today?
READ, READ, and READ some more. Read every thing you can get your hands on about the mortgage industry. Learn as many mortgage programs and options as you can. People want to do business with someone who they feel knows what they are doing.

Knowing what you know now, what would you have done differently in your mortgage career?
I would have started sooner. I spent many years as a real estate agent. I enjoyed real estate but you have much better control of your time in the mortgage industry.

Please describe your job description.
I am a branch manager and enjoy seeing the happy faces
of our satisfied customers.

*What one tool would you say is essential to a newcomer
in the business?*
PC skills

Is there any other advice you would give?
Stay in touch with the people you have helped. Keep
your name in front them monthly and you will see your
referrals increase dramatically.

Name: Mr. Shamun "Shamoon" Mahmud
Title: Mortgage Consultant
Organization: Allied Home Mortgage
Email: shamun.mahmud@520LOAN.com

How long have you been in the mortgage brokerage business?
One year

What do you like best about your job?
In a phrase, I love helping consumers live the American Dream. To see the joy in a person's eyes, when they take delivery of their home... Well, I still get a warm feeling.

What do you like least about your job?
Going back to the customer to ask for more information because "so-and-so" lender requires it for their new programs

What advice would you give a person starting today?
Begin personal marketing as soon as you get started in the field. Start networking with EVERYONE you know, whether they are business or personal contacts. Offer good advice asking nothing in return. Offer to consult people on their current loan offers from other companies. If they are good offers, tell them so and congratulate them on their savvy!

Knowing what you know now, what would you have done differently in your mortgage career?
Never compromise your ideals. Under promise and over deliver. I should have started sooner.

Please describe your job description.
Mortgage Consultant. I am more of a rainmaker than an LO.

What one tool would you say is essential to a newcomer in the business?
Act! database software.

Is there any other advice you would give?
Network with realtors. Start with introductory mail.
Follow up with voicemail broadcasts and faxes.

Name: Michael W. Schneiderman
Title: Senior Mortgage Consultant
Organization: Advanced Mortgage Solutions
Address: Highland Park, NJ
Email: mschnei244@aol.com

How long have you been in the mortgage brokerage business?
20 years

What do you like best about your job?
Being able to better explain the various programs to the client.

What do you like least about your job?
Sometimes, no matter how many times you explain the various products the client decides to take another one at a higher rate.

What advice would you give a person starting today?
Make sure that you fully understand the mortgage application (1003) and supported documents.

Knowing what you know now, what would you have done differently in your mortgage career?
Had a Web site sooner that would allow the individuals (potential customers) to see what is available.

Please describe your job description.
Senior mortgage consultant

What one tool would you say is essential to a newcomer in the business?
A mortgage calculator. Especially the HP 19B II which I have been using for over 20 years along with the printer.

Is there any other advice you would give?
Attend the various seminars in the field and keep talking to other mortgage bankers or brokers about the subject matter.

Name: Vida Bridges
Title: Loan Officer
Organization: Vida Bridges Brokerage Services
Email: vidabridges@aol.com

How long have you been in the mortgage brokerage business?
Two years

What is your yearly loan volume?
$1 million

What do you like best about your job?
Flexibility, the chance to help my clients repair their credit and get their financial life under control. Learning new things about the financial services industry

What do you like least about your job?
The lack of training from brokers, once you are signed up with them. Also how brokers give loan officers low commissions with little assistance. I was very frustrated throughout my career so far, but now I know the process and have begun to self-study.

What advice would you give a person starting today?
To learn the 1003 and how it controls the whole transaction. Get a copy of the stacking order for a file.

Develop a good team consisting of title companies, real estate agents, appraisers, lenders and veteran loan officers whom you can ask occasional questions.

Knowing what you know now, what would you have done differently in your mortgage career?
I would have studied marketing to get a good stream of clients. Do more research about companies (where you are thinking of working) and shadow them before signing up to see if there is a fit.

Please describe your job description.
Marketing to get customers, doing quick applications to see if the client will qualify, completing the 1003 loan application, running credit reports, getting loan approvals, doing title search, getting income document, bank statements, doing verifications, ordering appraisals, getting stipulations and closing loans

What one tool would you say is essential to a newcomer in the business?
Networking

Is there any other advice you would give?
I think this is a great thing to be doing. When I first started, I thought of it as a game. I could see the frustration on all of our faces. If it is a game, it can be fun from the beginning, instead of full of stress.

Name: Nicole Donn
Title: Branch Manager
Organization: US Financial Mortgage
Email: RELoan2000@aol.com

How long have you been in the mortgage brokerage business?
21 years

What is your yearly loan volume?
$24,000,000 -$40,000,000

What do you like best about your job?
I like being able to use my creativity to help people become homeowners and/or rearrange their finances so they are able to live more fully

What do you like least about your job?
I have been known to work way too many hours and I am not crazy about managing people.

What advice would you give a person starting today?
To learn as much as possible about the loan products. It should be easy to understand and if it is not, perhaps, this is not the right field for you. Also, every minute not working on a loan should be used to either learn about loans, self improvement or, most importantly, business development

Knowing what you know now, what would you have done differently in your mortgage career?
I would have screened out new loan officer recruits more carefully. I have wasted a lot of time training people who were not well suited for the job.

Please describe your job description.
I am the branch manager/owner/primary originator of a net branch

What one tool would you say is essential to a newcomer in the business?
Work hard networking with realtors and other business professionals until you have a reliable, consistent lead source. Stay in touch with existing customers.

Is there any other advice you would give?
Although the mortgage business is not for everyone, for those of us who have the aptitude, it is a great way to make a living. Do not bait and switch. Under promise and over deliver. This makes you look good and makes the transaction much less stressful. Be honest and don't gouge. Repeat and referral business is the easiest business to get and with the built in trust factor, the easiest business to close.

Name: Jeff Shaffer
Title: Loan Officer
Organization: Green Leaf Mortgage
Address: Montgomery Village, MD
Email: jeffshaffer00@yahoo.com

How long have you been in the mortgage brokerage business?
Two years

What is your yearly loan volume?
$12,000,000

What do you like best about your job?
Helping my clients

What do you like least about your job?
Dealing with over demanding Real Estate Agents

What advice would you give a person starting today?
Be very organized

Knowing what you know now, what would you have done differently in your mortgage career?
Started years ago!!

Please describe your job description.
Loan Officer--- Main function is to sell and close loans

What one tool would you say is essential to a newcomer in the business?
A strong loan processor

Is there any other advice you would give?
Only deal with lenders that are customer service oriented. We as loan officers have hundreds of choices of lenders. You must be very picky in choosing your lenders.

Name: Richelle McKim
Title: Mortgage Broker
Organization: Real Estate Mortgage Warehouse
Email: morningstarfin@juno.com

How long have you been in the mortgage brokerage business?
Eight months

What is your yearly loan volume?
$1,500,000.00

What do you like best about your job?
It's part-time. I can work it around my child.

What do you like least about your job?
On closing days, I might be on the phone 4 hours trying to baby-sit the details. It's hard to find a babysitter for a last-minute application or closing.

What advice would you give a person starting today?
Advertise once-a-month to every address you have. Use a title company's advertising department. Don't use cheesy materials. Give something to your customers that is valuable to them. Not just a recipe in the mail.

Knowing what you know now, what would you have done differently in your mortgage career?
Advertised more often

Please describe your job description.
Loan officer

What one tool would you say is essential to a newcomer in the business?
Learning the lingo, 10-o-3, (1003), etc. Hooking up with a good realtor, and being flexible.

Is there any other advice you would give?
Every closing ends up being a rush and no closing goes smoothly. Price your loans so that if your client goes to somebody else, the other mortgage broker will hardly make a dime, but price them so that you have some room to take out of your back-end for errors (pricing adjustments, lock extensions etc.)

Name: Dana D. Cubert
Title: Account Executive/ Loan Originator
Organization: Heartland Home Finance
Address: Indianapolis, In
Email: dcubert@heartlandfinance.com

How long have you been in the mortgage brokerage business?
4.5 years

What is your yearly loan volume?
Between 4-5 million

What do you like best about your job?
Helping customers save money on their mortgage refinancing. Getting to know my customers.

What do you like least about your job?
Not being able to help a customer who drastically needs financial relief on a monthly basis.

What advice would you give a person starting today?
Do not get frustrated. It is a killer to our line of business. Make sure you have a full pipeline (potential loans), because something will always come up when a loan officer is closing loans. Originate and originate. That is where you keep the stress to a minimum. Stress is unavoidable in our business.

Knowing what you know now, what would you have done differently in your mortgage career?
1. Took advantage of learning more products available with different lenders, and that would of been more money earned with each loan I touched.
2. Attached second mortgages and lines of credit with each first mortgage refinancing.

Debt relief is a seller for most first mortgage customers

Please describe your job description.
Loan originator, loan officer, account executive. And I have processed most of my own loans.

What one tool would you say is essential to a newcomer in the business?
Telephone, calculator, and scratch paper. Learn the business by scratch and not relying on a computer to get around in a loan

Is there any other advice you would give?
Originate, go out and see your customers, and learn all products available to you. This is your money and every customer is going to be doing a loan with someone.

It might as well be you. Be confident, and it will come out in you.

Name: Stacia Hamilton
Title: Mortgage Advisor
Organization: Equilliance Mortgage
Address: Orlando, Fl
Email: Stacia.Hamilton@equilliance.com

How long have you been in the mortgage brokerage business?
One year

What do you like best about your job?
Previously I was a Financial Advisor. I use this background to get a whole overview of what a person needs not just throw them into a mortgage. I enjoy helping people find the right mortgage to fit them and their new home.

What do you like least about your job?
I dislike the bad reputation many mortgage brokers have brought the business. There are a LOT of bad brokers out there throwing people into loans that will cause a foreclosure blowout in a year or two. I've watched too many brokers do it for the money and not for the client.

What advice would you give a person starting today?
I obtained my license in April of 2004, so as a newbie myself, I would advise someone to find a well established broker house. Here they would learn the in's and out's of basic mortgaging. They should also look for support and training because you learn nothing about mortgaging in the 3-day mortgage school. I would tell them to take a year or two to absorb as much as they could from the broker house and then look to move on. I wish someone would have told me this in the beginning. I started with a small mortgage company and I have tried to teach myself how to mortgage and have read as many books as I can on the subject, but without formal training it has taken me longer to get a "hang of the business" then it might

have otherwise. It's a lot more frustrating learning from mortgage to mortgage then to have a trainer or even a mentor. However, I would also warn them not to stay in a broker house too long as there are more exciting and interesting aspects to this job then what a broker house will teach you.

Knowing what you know now, what would you have done differently in your mortgage career?

1. Starting with a large company taking a smaller commission (50% of something is more than 70% of nothing)
2. Found a mentor
3. Started W2 (as a paid employee) and moved into 1099 (independent contractor)
4. Looked for support and training over commission
5. Set up a marketing campaign early on

Please describe your job description.
I write prescription mortgages to help ease home buying pain. We look at the whole financial picture along with the present and future plans and goals to prescribe the perfect mortgage for our clients.

What one tool would you say is essential to a newcomer in the business?
A mentor or trainer. The learning curve is so big in the beginning for this business it can be very overwhelming and intimidating. Having someone to turn to, to ask questions and get advice is essential to not only becoming a mortgage broker but surviving the first couple of years.

Is there any other advice you would give?
Just do it and hang in there. It's tough to get started but
easy once you get it. Also, network, network, network.
I attend at least 4 networking events a week to get my
name and face out there to the public. Go to leads groups,
happy hours, luncheons, special events, fundraisers,
social groups, and specific member meetings such as
women's groups, minority groups, religious groups, etc.
Just get out there and meet people, make referral partners
and get leads. The leads can turn into loans, which can
turn right back into referrals!!

Name: Steve Soccio
Title: Branch Manager
Organization: Louviers Mortgage Corporation
Address: Newark, DE

How long have you been in the mortgage brokerage business?
One year

What is your yearly loan volume?
3 million

What do you like best about your job?
Knowing that I am providing a resource to help people fulfill a dream of saving money or owning a home.

What do you like least about your job?
Having to decline potential clients

What advice would you give a person starting today?
Be prepared to do what it takes to become successful

Knowing what you know now, what would you have done differently in your mortgage career?
I would have spent more time on education and product development

Please describe your job description.
Being able to offer a convenient way to comparison shop for a loan in a secure, pressure-free environment. Consumers don't have to leave home or spend hours on the phone to get the best rates, because I will do all the legwork for them

What one tool would you say is essential to a newcomer in the business?
Dedication is the one tool that covers the amount of time you spend developing yourself, client base, education, and your overall success

Is there any other advice you would give?
Research the business completely. Every aspect of it.

Name: Donn S. Luthanen
Title: Branch Manager
Organization: Nationwide Equities Corp
Email: dluthanen@nwecorp.com

How long have you been in the mortgage brokerage business?
2.5 years

What do you like best about your job?
The ability to be creative through methods of problem solving to tailor loans to a PARTICULAR person(s) needs. Each person is different and methods need to be learned everyday to do the job correctly.

What do you like least about your job?
Knowing that there are plenty of people in the industry that have immoral practices. This creates great apprehension for clients to come over in the beginning of the mortgage process. The industry needs to pride itself on becoming recognized as a profession like doctors or lawyers.

What advice would you give a person starting today?
Be honest, learn your products, find computer software that speeds your process, and do not be greedy on one file to look for referrals. Learn to use veracity in all aspects of your business.

Knowing what you know now, what would you have done differently in your mortgage career?
1. I would have worked with a large company first to learn how and what I needed to create my business and goals.
2. I would have spent more time in the beginning on bringing new business to the table than structuring the office for "what might be."

Please describe your job description.
Manager: I over see all operations of the business. I pride myself on being compliant with the law and make sure the employees see the importance of it. I also educate them myself.

What one tool would you say is essential to a newcomer in the business?
A software program to database clients, a system to build referral sources from past clients (mailings or emails-Thank You Cards), a cell phone to be available whenever you can be. Only use a few lenders so you do not waste time looking for the best deal through 100s of places. Time is the most valuable asset you have.

Is there any other advice you would give?
Read the laws from the banking department. Go to websites for mortgage professionals and spend the time to read what other people are doing. Read product guidelines. BIGGEST TIP: DO NOT RELY ON OTHER PEOPLE FOR INFORMATION. Look it up yourself.

Marketing Materials You Need to Succeed

ATTENTION MORTGAGE BROKERS: NOT BEING PROPERLY TRAINED CAN COST YOU THOUSANDS IN LOST COMMISSIONS!

As a mortgage originator you make a living by writing up applications.

But you can never reach your true potential if you don't do it right.

Residential Mortgage Loan Origination Made Easy has been written to teach you how to originate loans and get them closed, so you can get paid more often.

Knowledge results in more confidence and more money. The better trained you are, the higher your tax bracket can be. Plus, borrowers flock to the individuals who are confident and who can answer their questions right away. Your referral business will skyrocket as your knowledge increases.

Put yourself in the borrower's shoes. Who would you do business with: a cool, confident professional, or a nervous rookie that cannot even answer basic questions?

YOU CANNOT AFFORD TO BE A ROOKIE

Not in this game. Because losing in this game means losing your house, your car and your job.

You have chosen to be a mortgage professional and that's what you need to be. The better trained you are the more professional you can be.

This Manual Gives You The Basic Mortgage Training You Need To Be Professional.

Over 180 pages of confidence building, image-enhancing material is within your grasp. Over 17 chapters that cover all you need to know to be the best mortgage originator around. Once you complete this manual, your co-workers who have been in business for years, will be amazed that you are more knowledgeable than they are!

This book is a must for all loan officers originating loans. It is both an excellent training manual and a wonderful reference book of mortgage laws, terms, and techniques. Not only is it filled with useful information, but you also get easy to use forms, agreements, and worksheets.

"When I first got my license, I was nervous before every conversation. I was afraid someone would ask me something that I didn't know. After reading your book, I now know what to say. I can now answers questions that used to trip me up and cost me loans. I found in your book what I did not find anywhere else. Thank you so much."

—Alan Sans, Detroit, Michigan

So how can you be a successful mortgage originator?

To Be A Successful Mortgage Originator There Are 3 Things You Must Know

Item 1: Know the laws and guidelines involved in mortgage originating.

Item 2: Know how to take an application, qualify and place a loan.

Item 3: Get the loan closed.

This book teaches you all three.

Item 1: Chapters 5-8 cover all the laws concerning your mortgage originations, as well as all <u>FNMA loan guidelines.</u>

Item 2: Chapters 9-13 teach you exactly what to do and what to say to customers from an initial meeting through pre-qualification and through application. <u>This includes a line-by-line explanation of both the Good Faith Estimate and the 1003 Loan Application.</u>

Item 3: Chapters 14-17 help you understand what else is involved to close the loan—from locking the loan, to ordering the appraisal, to sending out verifications, to how long it should all take. Everything is covered.

But how can you be sure that you will know what to do then the time comes?

Good Question.

That's what Section 4 is for. It contains two exercises taken from real life situations for you to complete.

"Even after 3 years in the business, I was still running into road blocks that kept my loans from closing. I had plenty of leads, but most of them did not qualify. That is, until I got your manual. You showed me exactly how to place my loans to get more of them approved. In the first three months after getting the manual, I closed 6 loans that I otherwise would have lost. That's $9,000 I would have been without!"

—Ryan Thomas, High Point, North Carolina

So what's left to know? Nothing.

This book will show you how to:

- Get your loans approved by FNMA.
- Do a full-fledged pre-qualification in less than 5 minutes.
- Fill out a Good Faith Application with your eyes closed.
- Complete an entire 1003 application and understand it thoroughly—this includes exercises.
- Complete all FNMA requirements for the property and the borrower.
- Use the tools you need to succeed in this business. You already have most of them, the rest you can get from this manual
- Know the differences between the various mortgage loans available today.
- Understand and interpret rate sheets.
- Obey all laws involved to keep you out of jail.
- Understand B, C, and D markets.
- Read a review of the most widely used mortgage products available today.

- Know the most frequently asked questions by borrowers and their answers.

  "Wow, I can't believe the stuff I didn't know about until I read a friend's copy of your training manual. I have to get one for myself."

  —Alonzo Santiago, Bolder Colorado

You will learn:

- Why being a mortgage originator is one of the last professions remaining that you can enter with little out of your pocket and unlimited income potential.
- What you will need to get started.
- Who should you work for—lender or broker—strengths and weaknesses of both are discussed.
- How and what wrong questions asked to a borrower can land you in serious trouble with the law.
- How the lending system works from the inside out—a thorough explanation of primary and secondary markets.
- Which laws affect mortgage origination and how to abide by them.
- How to lock a rate and explain its importance to borrowers.
- How to read and interpret a credit report.
- How appraisals are completed and the methods used.
- How long a mortgage should take to close and how long each step takes.
- Why people use mortgage brokers—and it's not the rate!
- The ins and outs of RESPA, Reg-Z, and ECOA.

Who is this book for?

The New Kid On The Block—for a jump-start in the business

The Old Pro—for an invaluable reference

The Training Manager—for a training supplement

The Processor—for an inside look at what loan officers know

The Real Estate Agent—for a tool to improve communication with loan officers and make sure everything is being done properly so the deals close.

Anyone Looking To Get Into The Business—for a behind- the-scenes look at what it's like and what to expect as well as detailed instructions on what to do once you are in the business.

> *"Your book is on the top shelf of my bookcase. I know exactly where it is whenever I need to look up something. Even after doing a few hundred loans, there is no way I am going to remember all the legal mumbo-jumbo. And I don't want to. So whenever I need to look up something, I just pick up your book. Make sure to contact me when it is updated."*
>
> —Lourdes Sanchez, Miami Florida

The Bottom Line...

Whether you are already in the mortgage business, or looking to get in, the information in this book will make you a Mortgage Origination Expert.

If you want to be a real professional mortgage loan originator, this book is for you.

Just check out the table of contents and see for yourself all that's included.

SECTION 1: SO YOU WANT TO BE A MORTGAGE LOAN ORIGINATOR?

SECTION 2: AN INTRODUCTION TO MORTGAGE LENDING

SECTION 3: IN THE FIELD

SECTION 4: LET'S SEE WHAT YOU GOT

Exercise 1

Exercise 2

Appendix 1: Disclosures

Appendix 2: Verification and Other Forms

Glossary

Before we send you to the order form, we wanted to let you know that along with the manual we are providing several

FREE BONUSES!

Bonus #1: Mortgage Broker Marketing On a Shoestring Budget—How To Jump Start Your Income As A Mortgage Broker For Less Than $200.

This FREE report details the most powerful methods of marketing known to the mortgage industry. We use all these techniques in our office every day. And they work. If you are looking for a way to have more leads than you can handle, use just a couple of the methods discussed in this report. It is jam packed with ideas that for under $200 can be implemented today.

We have seen marketing "gurus" charge hundreds of dollars for this same information. We ourselves charge $39.95 for this report by itself. You get it for FREE along with the manual. We want you to be super successful and we feel that the manual and the report put you head and shoulders above 95% of your competition.

Implementing just one of these methods will bring in enough in commissions to pay for the manual a thousand times.

We left nothing back. We put in everything you need to know. Even if you buy the manual just for this report, it is worth every penny and them some. You'll see.

Bonus #2: Secrets of the Richest People—Find out how the rich think—why they are more successful than other people, when they all have challenges and problems just everybody else. This FREE report will open your eyes. It helps you identify what you haven't done yet to be rich. It teaches you what you can do to BE rich. This is our motivational Bonus. It puts you in the right frame of mind to go out and implement the strategies we teach on the manual and Bonus #1.

Following our strategies, you will be armed with the information you need to make a lot of money in this business. But if your mind is not ready to handle it, you can sabotage your own efforts. There is a proper way to "think rich". This report shows you how. Sold by itself for $39.95, it is yours free.

Bonus #3: How to Influence People and Win Them Over—This FREE report details exactly what you need to do to attract more clients. The more people like you, the better your chances they will do business with you. So you need to know how to get through their "barriers" and into their good graces.

If you don't have a bubbly personality and aren't the star of every party you go to, you need this report.

One of the most important things of mortgage marketing is being remembered. This report will show you how to be remembered by everyone you meet. Sold by itself for $39.95, it is yours free.

Residential Mortgage Loan Origination Made Easy is distributed by Kamrock Publishing LLC, in consultation with MoneyTree Mortgage in Houston.

It was originally developed as a training manual for our brokers only. A couple years ago, one of our new brokers took the manual to a yearly convention of the Texas Association of Mortgage Brokers. At the convention, the manual was accidentally lost. It turned out that a head trainer from a larger company had picked it up and thumbed through it. After getting rave reviews from this person, we decided to share it with mortgage brokers nationwide.

"No one in my office could believe that I was able to make $9,000 on my first loan! But I did. And it's all thanks to what I got out of your book. Keep up the great work."

—Timothy Moore, Irvine California

"At first I thought you were asking too much for your manual. So I ordered one from someone else. Some of the information in that book was totally wrong and out of date. But I didn't know better so I did what that book said. Because of it, I got fired from the company I was at, and almost got sued by the borrower. I learned the hard way that it's better to pay a few extra dollars and get the best."

—Author asked for name not to be revealed.

Up until now we haven't told you how much it is.

Take a look at what is being offered and make a guess as to how much this book is worth to you. It can take years off your learning curve if you are new in the business.

The average loan you make should net you about $2000. You will definitely get one more loan from the material in the manual and the FREE REPORTS.

If you sat through a seminar that covered all this material, it would take at least 3 days. That is how long it takes us to cover all this material when training new brokers. How much is your time worth?

How about the loans you could lose if you don't get this information? One broker earned $9000 within a few months because of what he learned from this manual.

We could easily charge a few hundred dollars and it would still be a bargain.

But in order the make it affordable to all brokers we have lowered the cost to only $199.99. Oops. That's a typo. It should be $137.

You get the complete 180+ page manual, the jam packed Free Reports, and our unconditional 30-day money back guarantee.

THE GUARANTEE

We want you to be a Mortgage Origination Pro. We're only happy if you are really happy. So here's our guarantee to you.

If you feel that Residential Mortgage Loan Origination Made Easy does not deliver everything we say it does, simply tell us you want your money back within 30 days.

We'll refund your money immediately. And you get to keep the FREE Reports!

- No reason required
- No exceptions
- No strings attached

"I've worked in the mortgage industry for ten years. I first saw your manual about three years ago, and knew right away it was simply the best manual of its kind in the marketplace. Today, when I hire a new broker, the first thing I do is make them read through your entire manual. Doing this has saved me countless hours of training them. Keep up the good work. "

—Mike Tong, Baltimore MD

"Where were you guys when I first started? It took me 3 years to learn everything my son learned by reading your manual in two days! "

—Russell White, Dayton OH

"I just got my license two weeks before getting your manual, and I didn't have a clue of what to do first. Thank God your sales letter got to me. Because of your manual, I stopped myself from making a couple huge mistakes: 1. Working for the wrong company and 2. How to market without spending lots of money. Thank you so much!"

—Yammy Rodriguez, Miami Florida

"I have worked at 5 different mortgage companies in the past 8 years. And I know of no one who knows more about mortgage origination than Abby Kamadia. I thought I knew a lot when I came to work for him. But he blew me away. And he has put everything you need to know into this manual. There is nothing that you can do that will help your career better than to read this thing cover to cover. Just do it."

—A Aribani, Houston Texas

"I wish all brokers sending me loans had this manual. I spend most of my day fixing items in files that have been submitted wrongly and answering basic questions by untrained brokers. Please Abby, just give it away to everyone!"

—Eddy Osborn, Wholesale Lending Division, National Lender

REMEMBER OUR PROMISE:

You will close more loans or your money back

Yours in success,
Abby Kamadia
MoneyTree Mortgage

P.S. A six figure income starts with one simple step – Being committed to yourself and ordering this manual. ORDER TODAY!

TO ORDER:

By Phone: Call us at 713-782-5626. Have your credit card ready.

Online: www.mortgagebrokertraining.com

By Mail: Mail your check or money order to:

Kamrock Publishing
7447 Harwin St, Suite 218
Houston, TX 77036

How To Get An Enthusiastic "YES!" From Realtors, Every Time You Ask For Business.

Working with just one average Realtor can put over $40,000 in your pocket year after year!

Read on to learn how you can get DOZENS of them to call you:

- **without cold calling,**
- **without rejection,**
- **without donuts**
- **and without rate sheets.**

A Realtor called me the other day and you won't believe what he said,

> *"Mr. Kamadia, another agent in my office works with you, and she told me this morning how she no longer has to spend any time following up on her leads. She also said how her business has increased as a direct result of working with you. I did over 4 million in sales last year and I would love to meet with you and discuss how we can work together."*

He would never have called me, if it weren't for my simple, easy to use, almost-no-work-involved marketing system.

My system gets dozens of Realtors to call me wanting me to help them increase their business. And because I help them make more money, they give me all their loans and leads. You can easily do the same thing I do.

My new system of getting Realtor business has been so successful, I had to hire another assistant!

I call my system, **The Marketing To Realtors Toolkit.** It's called a Toolkit because it has everything you need to attract, convert, and get business from Realtors.

What makes the Toolkit so successful is simple: I give Realtors what they want, so they give me what I want.

Sit up straight and pay attention now, because here's the key: I offer Realtors something they want. They call me to get it. And when I give them what I promised, I show them something else; something that they cannot live without—and which they can only have, IF they work with me.

When they see what I have to offer, their eyes light up like 10 year-olds in a toy store, because they know it could easily double or triple their income in a few months.

And a recent survey by the National Association of Realtors shows again why it is so important for mortgage brokers and lenders to work with Realtors:

69% of all homebuyers in 2003 asked their Realtor to suggest a mortgage lender And 36% of all homebuyers chose their lender based only on the Realtor's recommendation.

In other words, if you're not working with Realtors you're missing at least 4 out of 10 homebuyers. And then you have to fight your competition for the rest.

Working with only one Realtor who gives you only one measly loan a month will result in over $40,000 in commissions a year! **Using this system you can easily work with 10, 20, 30 or more Realtors.**

If you have ever been rejected by a Realtor, keep reading.

Look how easy it is to use the Toolkit. (NO DONUTS OR RATE SHEETS)

Step 1: Use my ads or letters to offer Realtors an information filled "package" that will show them "How to Double Their Income in 90 Days".

Step 2: Once they call you to get this information (no cold-calling), you use the scripts provided to arrange a meeting with the Realtor in which you give them the "package."

Step 3: In the meeting, you use the other set of scripts included to explain to them the benefits of your "Client Follow-Up System."

Most Realtors do a decent amount of business but still struggle to get customers because they suck at marketing and doing proper follow up. Instead of waiting for them to learn, I take it upon myself to do it for them. And to make this as simple and effortless as possible, I created a complete "Client Follow-Up System" that separates potential homebuyers into three categories: (1) the credit challenged, (2) the down payment impaired, and (3) those who want to buy, but just don't want to buy right now.

Step 4. The Realtors fall in love with my system, (especially since it is Free for them), and start providing leads to enter into it.

This helps the Realtor, because they never lose track of another lead. Every lead is properly followed up with. And every lead, which makes it through the system is sent back to the Realtor to buy a house.

And, when you are using my Toolkit, this helps you because:

- From the Realtors, you get loans from all the clients who are ready to buy now

- You get a ton of leads from your Realtors
- A whopping 99% of the leads which make it through the system will get their loan from you.
- Your pipeline is always full
- You can predict how many loans you will have every month
- Your marketing costs are almost zero
- You get many, many referrals from the buyers who go through the system
- Your Realtors refer you other Realtors to work with

The entire "Client Follow-Up System" is also part of the Toolkit. Just plug the leads you get into the system and let to do its work. You and your Realtor partners will be amazed at how the system increases both your businesses.

Step 5. If the Realtor is someone you want to work with, but does not agree to work with you right away, (probably because he is already happy with another lender), you use my 100 contact "Realtor Follow-Up" process to stay in touch and eventually win him over.

Here are the early results:

The first month I implemented the system I describe in the Toolkit, I went on 26 Realtor interviews. (All of them had called me to ask for meetings). Before that time, I had never been to meet a Realtor before. Out of those 26 meetings, 20 eventually agreed to work with me. From those 20, **in three months, I got 22 loans.** And that is not counting all the leads that were given to me which will materialize into loans in the future.

(To be honest, not every one of these Realtors was worth working with, but since this was the first time I tried the system, I went to see every Realtor that called me. Now, I pre-qualify the Realtors before I meet them. And if they don't do enough business, I don't bother with them.)

That is the power the Toolkit can give you...

You will be able to turn away Realtors who want to work with you. (But only if you want to.)

It only took 3 months to get 22 loans. And since everything you need is in the Toolkit, you can set up the whole thing in a couple days.

Some important reasons why you'll want to try The Marketing To Realtors Toolkit for yourself:

1. Anyone can duplicate my results. There is nothing in the Toolkit that takes a college education, or even much money to implement. It is a simple concept, fine tuned into a well-oiled, loan-producing machine. In fact, **in the manual I use an example of how you can start getting loans with only $500**.

2. You can be up and running in days. I have already spent the time developing and testing the whole process, and I turn it over to you. All you do is transfer the files from CD to your computer, place an ad, or mail a letter, and go meet Realtors when they call you. The laziest mortgage broker in the country can be generating phone calls in less than one week.

3. The Toolkit will help you meet and exceed all your income goals. Even if each Realtor gives you only one measly loan a month, how many Realtors do you need to be happy? Whatever your answer is, I promise to show you how to reach that level.

4. **The Toolkit will turn you into a Realtor Magnet. You will be able to attract Realtors to you like ants to a picnic**. You can gain the confidence and loyalty of as many Realtors as you can handle.

5. **You have no risk.** Try the Toolkit for yourself, and if you don't like it, you have one year to send it back for a complete refund. **A Full, One-Year Guarantee**. I only do this because I know it will work for you.

WHAT ARE SOME OF THE BENEFITS OF THE MARKETING TO REALTORS TOOLKIT?

- You will have a steady stream of loans each and every month from your Realtor Partners.

- You will no longer be dependant upon Realtors to send you business. Realtors will see you as a real partner and will even become dependant upon you!

- You will be in control of your business and life by having so many leads and loans. You will only work with the people who want to work with you.

- You will not need to spend money on consumer marketing because you will be able to capture 40% of homebuyers before they even talk to any other lender. Each Realtor should send you at least 2 loans per month. And you can easily convert 3-4 Realtors per month to work with you!

- You will not have to write, create, or spend time or money developing. Everything you need is included.

- You will eliminate the need to compete with other lenders, because borrowers will be sent to you already pre-sold on the idea of working with you.

- You will not have to change or stop doing anything you already do, just add this to it.

The next time you go to a real estate office, be an invited guest, instead of an unwanted pest.

HERE IS WHAT YOU GET IN THE TOOLKIT:

1. The instruction manual that gives you the details on how to use and implement the system. The manual helps you set up your game plan, decide on your marketing budget, choose the marketing method to use, and guides you through the Toolkit, step-by-step.

2. The marketing pieces you use to get Realtors to call you.

3. The scripts you use to get Realtors to agree to a meeting with you in order to discuss the information you are offering.

4. The actual "package" that is delivered to the Realtors. The "package" contains three separate reports dealing with different ways Realtors can improve their business, as well as other inserts that promote you as the only broker they need to work with.

5. The scripts to conduct the meeting and to introduce the "Client Follow-Up System".

6. The entire "Client Follow-Up System" for three different types of homebuyers, and over 25 contacts for each type to be used over a 6 month period of time.

7. An entire separate 100 contact "Realtor Follow-Up" system to use on those that do not agree to work with you right away.

8. All the ads, letters, scripts, and all the contacts on a separate CD so all you have to do is save them to your computer.

It takes my assistant about 3 hours a week to implement the "Client Follow Up System" for all the leads my Realtors give us every week. They get these leads from phone inquiries, their own marketing, open houses, referrals, etc. Anyone that wants to buy a house but is not ready to go looking right now is put into the system, until they are ready to buy.

And the Realtors love to do it. Mainly because they know they themselves do not follow up properly.

Almost overnight, my pipeline was full of these leads. Not all of them make it through the 6 month follow-up process, but my numbers show that 35% of all the leads handed to us, turn into a loan for me. The more Realtors I get, the more leads I get, and the more loans they send me from their "hot" buyers.

But I don't even count the leads. I look at them as gravy, frosting on the cake, an added bonus for me. Just because I am helping the Realtors, they in-turn refer ALL their homebuyers and sellers to me to get their loan. And it has dramatically helped my business!

I started getting so many new loans, I had to hire another assistant to handle the workload.

In addition to everything mentioned above I have added some FREE Bonuses to help you get the most from the Toolkit:

1. The actual "package" that I deliver to potential Realtors so you can see how I lay it out, how the insides are printed, and what is included.

2. The electronic version of the all time marketing classic book, *Scientific Advertising*, by Claude Hopkins. This book is considered by many of today's top marketers as the greatest book of all time written on the subject of advertising. This classic is so hard to get, bookstores even have a hard time keeping it in stock, if they can get it at all.

3. The electronic version of the best-selling book, *How To Make Your Credit Sparkle*. This was the first book to detail the actual score factors the credit bureaus use to determine credit scores. It has helped thousands understand and improve their credit. Currently on sale for $37, it is yours FREE.

4. The electronic version of the book *The Science of Getting Rich*. This powerful manual of wealth building gives the essential secrets of being rich. It gets to the core of how anyone can become wealthy. It is also yours FREE.

5. A CD with all the letters, scripts, marketing pieces, each contact of the Customer Follow-Up System, and each contact in the Realtor Follow-up System, so you can easily load them on your computer. You don't need to change a thing. Just add your name and you are set to go.

Creating the Toolkit, took me countless hours, and several thousand dollars. But it was worth it. **Just one Realtor giving you just one loan a month, will earn you over $40,000 in one year.** And in the few short months since I started using the systems, I already cemented relationships with many Realtors who do much, much better than that.

My price to you for the entire Marketing To Realtors Toolkit, and Free bonuses is a paltry $499. Heck if you get just one loan, you'll make enough to buy a Toolkit for everyone in your office. And remember, I will let you keep and use the Toolkit for a full year. If it does not turn you into a Realtor Magnet where Realtors are dying to work with you, send it back for a full refund.

Sincerely,
Abby Kamadia
V.P. MoneyTree Mortgage

You can order by:

1. Calling my office at 713-782-5626
2. Visiting the website **www.marketingtoRealtors.com**

Give your business a quantum leap. ORDER TODAY!

P.S. A One-Year Guarantee! You have nothing to lose. This offer WILL NOT last long.

P.P.S. If you want Realtor business without having to bother with rate sheets, donuts, or buying lunches, you gotta get this thing!

P.P.P.S. I would hate for someone else in your market to get the Toolkit before you do and get all the Top Producing Realtors before you. So order right now!

Your Next Step

The following tools will help you start your mortgage career on the right foot. They have been developed with new brokers in mind. Not only will they help you take years off your learning curve, but they will also help you start earning money from Day 1.

It's a sad fact that not everyone becomes successful as a mortgage broker. The difference between the top producers and the failures is knowledge. This same knowledge is now available to you. Use it from the beginning of your career and you will never have to look back.

HERE'S A PARTIAL LIST OF WHAT YOU NEED TO CHECK INTO:

Referrals On Demand - Generate loans on Day 1 of your mortgage career. Referrals are the easiest and best loans to get. Learn the secrets to get your customers to refer you to everyone they know. This won't happen automatically unless you use the systems revealed in this system. There is no other marketing system on the market that is guaranteed to bring results like this one.

Jump Start Your Mortgage Career – This intensive e-class will go through everything you need to know to start quickly and grow fast. Whether you are brand new or in a slump, this class will teach you how customers think, how to attract them in droves, and how to build a business that will last for years.

One-on-One Coaching Program – Even Michael Jordan had a coach his entire career. Now you can learn from the best of the best. Ameen Kamadia – author of this book provides coaching to a limited few. But you must qualify.

The Millionaire Loan Officer Newsletter – What the Top Producers read. This monthly newsletter provides the most up-to-date marketing strategies that are working in the field for other loan officers. Each issue is jam-packed with mind-blowing ideas, business building strategies, and life-changing revelations.

To learn more about these and all our other products visit:

WWW.MORTGAGEBROKERTRAINING.COM